Understanding Traditional Stories

Differentiated Comprehension and Reading Activities for KS1 Using Retellings of Stories from Around the World

Brilliant
PUBLICATIONS

Karen Moncrieffe

We hope you and your pupils enjoy the activities in this book. Brilliant Publications publishes many other books to support, inspire and challenge primary school teachers and pupils. To find out more details on any of our titles please log onto our website: www.brilliantpublications.co.uk.

Understanding Myths and Legends Years 7–11
Reading Comprehension, 2nd Edition Year 1 and Year 2
Phonic Limericks with Zöe Zebra and Friends
Phonic Limerick Friends
Creative Writing, Year 1 and Year 2
Grammar and Punctuation, Year 1 and Year 2
Boost Creative Writing Skills Ages 5–7
Where Can an Elephant Hide? Challenges to Ignite Learning in Key Stage 1
43 Team-building Activities for Key Stage 1

~~~~~~

Published by Brilliant Publications
Unit 10,
Sparrow Hall Farm,
Edlesborough,
Dunstable,
Bedfordshire,
LU6 2ES

Website: www.brilliantpublications.co.uk
E-mail: info@brilliantpublications.co.uk
Tel: 01525 222292
Fax: 01525 222720

The name 'Brilliant Publications' and the logo are registered trade marks.

Written by Karen Moncrieffe
Illustrated by Molly Sage
Cover illustration by Molly Sage

© 2015 Karen Moncrieffe and Brilliant Publications
Printed ISBN: 978-1-78317-146-0
e-pdf ISBN: 978-1-78317-147-7
First published 2015
10 9 8 7 6 5 4 3 2 1

~~~~~~

Karen Moncrieffe is an experienced primary school teacher and a former literacy co-ordinator. She currently teaches in Birmingham. Karen has produced a variety of resources for teachers to use to develop their pupils' reading and writing skills. She loves both writing and teaching, and is passionate about helping pupils to develop a love of literacy.

Visit her website **www.primarytexts.co.uk.**

Contents

Introduction..4
How to Use this Book 5–6

Fables
The Wind and the Sun (Greece)..7–10
The Ant and the Grasshopper (Greece)...11–14
Hare and the Tortoise (Greece) 15–18
The Miller, his Son and the Donkey (Greece) 19–22
The Tale of Two Fishes and a Frog (India) 23–26
The Flying Turtle (India) 27–30
The Singing Donkey (India) 31–34

Folk Stories
Abu Ali Counts his Donkeys (Middle East) 35–38
Rabbit Catches the Sun (America)..39–42
The Giant Turnip (Russia) 43–46
The Greedy Lion (Africa) 47–50
Tortoise and Baboon (Africa) 51–54
The Fox and the Tiger (China)..55–58
The Lion and the Jackal (Africa) 59–62
The Fox and the Bagpipes (Scotland) 63–66
Why the Emu has Short Wings (Australia)...67–70
The Lizard and the Sun (Mexico) 71–74

Fairy Tales
The Elves and the Shoemaker (Germany) 75–79
The Gingerbread Man (America)...80–84
The Magic Porridge Pot (Germany) 85–88
The Three Billy Goats Gruff (Norway) 89–92
The Ugly Duckling (Denmark)..93–97
Cinderella (France) 98–102
Goldilocks and the Three Bears (England) 103–107
The Three Little Pigs (England)...108–113

Introduction

Traditional stories and tales have been passed on from generation to generation through word of mouth and in this book we are striving to retell them in a format suitable for KS1 children. For the purposes of this book, the term traditional stories, encompasses fables, folk stories and fairy tales.

Fables are short stories which usually involve animals, and have a specified or obvious moral. The selected folk stories are also quite short and are often amusing in tone with a less clearly defined moral. The selected fairy tales are mostly from well-known collections including Andersen, Grimm and Perrault.

The stories in this book are from countries from across the globe. Storytelling is an art that has been practised in every culture throughout history. Long before people could write, stories were told.

The main purpose of traditional stories is to teach and explain. They contain lessons about how to behave towards others, and they teach children what they need to do to achieve success. Many of these stories contain implicit (or sometimes explicit) morals and lessons.

Children reading these stories today may also learn valuable lessons about the importance of respecting others, and about the differences between cultures and religions. In addition to this, these tales and stories are often enjoyable and funny, with clever characters and amusing endings; which encourage children to develop a love of stories and reading.

On occasion, some traditional stories have fallen out of fashion. Do fairy tales teach us that passivity in females is a good trait? Do they reinforce the ideas that only boys can be clever and strong? Do they place too much emphasis on the importance of physical beauty rather than inner qualities? Teachers should be prepared to discuss and debate any unsuitable hidden messages with children, even at infant level. However, despite the fact that it could be argued that there are issues with the underlying messages of some traditional stories, these stories are almost certainly destined to remain a part of the school curriculum.

So why do traditional stories and tales have such enduring appeal? Traditional stories and tales from around the world contain universal themes. The most prominent theme is that of good prevailing over evil. They also show the importance of perseverance, striving to overcome challenges and illustrate that clever thinking can help us to master problems. Not only do these stories help us to learn, but they are also very entertaining and more importantly, children enjoy hearing and reading them.

Centuries ago, children were being told the very same stories that we share with our children today. This tradition is likely to continue well into the future. It is fascinating to consider that the traditional stories contained in the pages of this book will probably be told to children across the world for many years to come.

How to Use this Book

This teacher resource book contains fables, folk stories and fairy tales from many countries around the world. It is a very flexible resource and is suitable for use in literacy lessons. The stories and activities are also ideal for use in shared and guided reading sessions. In addition to these uses, teachers might find the stories useful for assemblies. Many of the *Follow-up Activities* have links to other curriculum areas, such as science.

Each story is accompanied by:

- A section containing 'Words to Discuss Before Reading'
- A 'Speaking and Listening Activity' to be used after reading
- Follow-up Activities
- Differentiated 'Reading Tasks' listed from A to D.

Teachers should judge whether they think the reading level of the text is suitable for their pupils. If not, they may choose to simply share and discuss the story with the children and support them with the associated activities. Some stories are more complex than others.

Many of the fairy tales are longer than the selected folk stories and fables, so teachers may feel they need to support the children more with these. With longer fairy tales, the beginning of the story is followed by the comprehension activities. After completing the activities, there is an opportunity for children to finish the story. This is obviously particularly important for those children who may not be familiar with the story, and do not know what happens at the end. After completing the story, teachers could follow-up by asking the children to talk or write about their favourite parts, describe characters or express their opinion of the ending.

The *Words to Discuss Before Reading* section contains words the children will encounter during the story which may be new to them. Before reading, teachers should explain and discuss the meaning of these words. This will help children to build on their vocabulary and help aid their comprehension of the story.

The aims of the *Speaking and Listening Activity* is to deepen the children's insight and to encourage engagement. The book contains a range of suggested activities which are explained in the teaching notes for each story. To increase depth of understanding, it is a good idea for pupils to do the speaking and listening activities after reading the story, but prior to doing the reading tasks.

The *Reading Tasks* are differentiated; therefore they are suitable for children of different ages and abilities. Questions are of varying styles and should be used in order to help to improve the children's general reading and comprehension abilities.

- ◆ *Task A* activities require the children to complete or rearrange words in sentences so that they read correctly and make sense. These tasks involve straight forward information retrieval.

◆ *Task B* activities are drawing tasks. Children need to be able to visualise elements from the story, refer to the text and use their imagination.

◆ For *Task C* activities, children need to think more carefully. There are some information retrieval questions which require the children to work more independently. There are also sequencing activities, true/false questions, matching activities and multiple choice.

◆ *Task D* activities require deeper thought. Activities include expressing their opinions and answering more complex questions. They may need to use inference and deduction skills and make reference to the text.

Teachers may choose to give pupils task A and B or C and D, or expect the children to complete all tasks, dependent on the pupil's age, ability and the lesson structure.

Follow-up Activities are varied and cross curricular. Through these activities children can extend and deepen their understanding. Teachers may choose to take a thematic approach and use the stories as a stimulus to develop work with the whole class in other curriculum areas.

Morals linked to the fables are included on the appropriate pages.

The Wind and the Sun

The Wind and the Sun were having an argument about which one of them was the strongest. As they argued, they saw a man walking down the road. They both agreed on an idea.

"Let's see who can make this man take off his coat," they decided. "That will show which one of us is the strongest."

"You go first," said the Sun.

The Wind blew so hard that leaves were whipped away from the trees. But this made the man clutch his coat more tightly. Next, it was the Sun's turn. The Sun shone brightly. The man felt so hot that he took off his coat.

The Sun won!

Understanding Traditional Stories

Teacher's Notes: The Wind and the Sun

Background Information
One of Aesop's fables from Ancient Greece.

Words to Discuss Before Reading

argument when two people think differently about something and tell each other what they think, sometimes in an angry way. Both people might try to persuade each other that they are right.

idea to think of a way to do something or to solve a problem.

clutch to hold onto something tightly.

Speaking and Listening Activity
After reading, ask the children to imagine what the man might have been thinking when the wind was blowing. They could role-play this part of the story with the actors speaking their thoughts out loud. Next, the children could repeat the activity for the following part of the story when the sun is shining.

Follow-up Activities

◆ The children could sketch pictures showing what they would wear, both on a sunny day and a windy day.

◆ Explain that wind strength can be measured using the Beaufort scale. Find pictorial images which represent the Beaufort scale. Ask the children to discuss in pairs which picture they think would match the wind strength today. They could then decide which picture might best represent the strength of the wind when it blew in the story.

The Wind and the Sun

Reading Task A Write the words in the correct order.

1.   hard. blew The Wind

_____

2.   The brightly. Sun shone

_____

3.   hot. man felt The

_____

4.   Sun The won!

_____

Reading Task B Draw a picture which shows the part of the story when the Wind was blowing.

The Wind and the Sun

Reading Task C Circle the correct answer.

1. The Wind argued with the
   a) Moon. b) Sun. c) rain. d) sky.

2. They saw a man walking down the
   a) rain. b) rocks. c) road. d) row.

3. The Wind and the Sun tried to get the man to take off his
   a) hat. b) coat. c) shoes.

4. The man took off his coat because
   a) the Wind blew. b) the Sun was hot.

Reading Task D Write what you think.

1. Explain why the Wind could not manage to make the man take off his coat.

_____

_____

2. Do you prefer sunny weather or windy weather? Explain why.

_____

_____

_____

_____

Understanding Traditional Stories

The Ant and the Grasshopper

It was a hot summer's day. A grasshopper played around singing, jumping and enjoying itself in the sun. An ant walked past carrying a grain of wheat.

"That looks like hard work," said the grasshopper.

"I'm gathering food for the winter," said the ant. "You should do the same."

The grasshopper took no notice. When winter came, the grasshopper was hungry. He searched for food but could not find any. He went to look for the ant and begged him to share his food.

"No!" shouted the ant. "You should have listened to me."

Teacher's Notes:
The Ant and the Grasshopper

Background Information
One of Aesop's fables from Greece.

Words to Discuss Before Reading

grasshopper   Ask if any of the children know what a grasshopper is. Show them pictures of a grasshopper. Discuss facts about grasshoppers, for example they can leap about twenty times the length of their body and they 'sing' by rubbing their back legs or wings together.

gathering   Explain that in the story this means collecting food.

grain of wheat   Show pictures of a grain of wheat. Explain that wheat is grown in fields by farmers and that it is a form of food. You could elaborate by explaining that we use it to make bread.

Speaking and Listening Activities
After reading, refer back to the part of the story where the grasshopper begs the ant for food. What might the ant have said? Ask the children to pretend they are the grasshopper. What might they say to the ant to try to convince him to give them food?

Follow-up Activities

◆   Support the children in finding out more about how ants behave.

◆   Help the children to investigate how different animals cope in the winter, eg, squirrels, birds, hedgehogs.

Moral
It is not good to play all of the time.

The Ant and the Grasshopper

Reading Task A — Write the words in the correct order.

1. played. The grasshopper

_____

2. The worked ant hard.

_____

3. food. grasshopper any find could not The

_____

4. hungry. The grasshopper was

_____

Reading Task B — Draw pictures that show what it is like outside in winter and outside in summer.

The Ant and the Grasshopper

Reading Task C Circle True or False.

1. It was a cold summer day.   True/False

2. The ant carried a grain of wheat.   True/False

3. The grasshopper collected food.   True/False

4. The grasshopper wanted the ant to share.
                                                True/False

5. The ant shared with the grasshopper.   True/False

Reading Task D Write what you think.

1. Describe how the ant behaved.

_____

2. Describe how the grasshopper behaved.

_____

3. Do you think the ant should have shared his food with the grasshopper? Explain your answer.

_____

Understanding Traditional Stories

The Hare and the Tortoise

There once lived a hare who loved to boast.

"I am the best at everything!" he would say.

One day a tortoise heard him boasting.

"I bet I could beat you in a race," said the tortoise.

"Don't be silly!" said the hare. "You could never beat me!"

They set a date for a race, and the day came. The hare was so confident that during the race, he decided to lie down and have a nap. Tortoise passed him while he was sleeping. When the hare woke up, he found out that Tortoise had won the race!

Teacher's notes: The Hare and the Tortoise

Background Information
One of Aesop's fables from Ancient Greece.

Words to Discuss Before Reading:

boasting — when someone speaks very proudly about something they can do to the point of showing off. Discuss whether it is right or wrong to 'show off'.

confident — feeling very sure that you are able to do something. Ask the children to discuss the things they feel confident about.

decide — to choose to do something.

steady — to keep going calmly at the same speed, without slowing down or speeding up.

Ask the children to imagine someone walking in a steady way. How might this look? If there is space they could demonstrate.

Speaking and Listening Activities
After reading, ask the children to describe how they think the hare felt when he reached the finish line and found out the tortoise was already there. What might the conversation have been? What might the hare have said to the tortoise? What do they think that the tortoise would have said back? In pairs role-play this conversation.

Follow-up Activities

◆ Imagine the tortoise was given a certificate for winning the race. What might it look like? What might be written on it? Make a certificate for the tortoise to say well done for winning the race.

◆ The tortoise and the hare had a running race. What other sorts of races are there? Ask the children to think about sports day and list some of the different races and events.

Moral
Slow and steady wins the race.

The Hare and the Tortoise

Reading Task A — Fill in the missing words.

best	nap	tortoise	race	won

1. The t _ _ _ _ _ _ _ heard the hare boasting.

2. The hare thought he was the b _ _ _ at everything.

3. The tortoise said that he could beat the hare in a
   r _ _ _ .

4. The hare had a n _ _ .

5. Tortoise w _ _ the race.

Reading Task B — Draw a picture which shows the tortoise passing the hare while the hare naps.

The Hare and the Tortoise

Reading Task C Write these events in the correct order.

The hare had a nap.
The hare and the tortoise had a race.
The tortoise won the race.

_____

_____

_____

_____

Reading Task D Write what you think.

1. How do you think the hare felt at the end of the race?
    Explain why.

    _____

    _____

2. How do you think the tortoise felt at the end of the story?
    Explain why.

    _____

    _____

3. What lesson do you think the hare learned in this story?

    _____

    _____

The Miller, his Son and the Donkey

A miller and his son walked to market with a donkey they planned to sell. They passed an old man who said:

"How silly of you both to walk - one of you should ride on the donkey!"

So the miller told his son to ride on the donkey. Next, they passed an old lady who said:

"Lazy boy! Get down and let your dad ride!"

The boy got down, and the miller climbed onto the donkey. Soon, they passed a young man who shouted:

"Lazy man! Get down and let your son ride!"

The miller did not know what to do. He decided it would probably be best if both he and his son rode on the donkey. But then, they passed a young lady who yelled:

"How selfish! That poor little donkey can't carry both of you!"

"Maybe no one will say anything if we both carry the donkey," thought the miller.

So the miller and his son picked up the donkey and carried him to the market. When they arrived, everyone pointed and laughed at the strange sight. Terrified by the noise, the donkey jumped from their arms straight into a river – and drowned.

"I wish we had not tried to listen to everyone," said the miller sadly.

Teacher's Notes:
The Miller, his Son and the Donkey

Background Information
One of Aesop's fables from Ancient Greece.

Words to Discuss Before Reading
miller   a person whose job is to grind (crush) grain to make flour. This is then often used to make bread.

probably   a good chance that something will happen.

terrified   very, very scared.

Speaking and Listening Activities
Ask the children what they might have done if they were in the miller or his son's position. Were they right to keep trying to listen to everyone? What do they think was the best way for the miller and his son to get to market with the donkey? Encourage each child to express their opinion and explain their thoughts. Do they all agree? Ask the children whether they think it is okay for people to have different opinions.

Follow-up Activities
◆   The children could find out more about donkeys. How are they used? What is the difference between a donkey and a horse?

◆   After completing the Speaking and Listening Activities, discuss the ending of the story. Starting from the point just after the young lady yells at the miller and his son, ask the children to rewrite the ending of the story changing it so that it ends in a happier way.

The Miller, his Son and the Donkey

Reading Task A Choose the correct word from the box below to complete the sentences.

selfish	boy	everyone	man	silly

1. The old man said, "How s _ _ _ _ _ _!"

2. The old lady said, "Lazy b _ _!"

3. The young man shouted, "Lazy m _ _!"

4. The young lady yelled, "How s _ _ _ _!"

5. The miller said, "I wish we hadn't listened to
   e _ _ _ _ _ _ _ _."

Reading Task B Draw the miller and his son carrying the donkey.

The Miller, his Son and the Donkey

Reading Task C Write these events in the correct order.

The miller and his son rode the donkey.

The miller rode the donkey.

The son rode the donkey.

_____

_____

_____

_____

Reading Task D Write what you think.

1. Did you think it was right when both the miller and his son rode on the donkey together? Explain why.

_____

_____

2. Why did everyone laugh at the miller and his son when they arrived at the market? Explain.

_____

_____

3. Why was the miller sad at the end? Explain.

_____

_____

The Tale of Two Fishes and a Frog

Long ago in a lake, there lived two fishes and a frog. They were great friends. One day two men came past and noticed the fishes.

"I didn't know there were fish in this lake," said one of the men. "Let's come back tomorrow with a fishing net and catch some food for dinner."

After the men left, the frog was very upset.

"We need to leave. It's too dangerous to stay!" he said.

But the fishes did not care – they just laughed at him.

"We're staying right here – those men will never be able to catch us!" they insisted.

The frog hopped away, leaving his friends in the lake. The next day, the frog watched sadly from a distance as the men came back with nets, and quickly caught both of the fish.

Understanding Traditional Stories

Teacher's Notes:
The Tale of Two Fishes and a Frog

Background Information
A fable from the Panchatantra: India.

Words to Discuss Before Reading
dangerous   something that could cause you harm, or injure you.
insisted   to say something in a strong firm way, believing that you are right.
distance   far away.

Speaking and Listening Activities
After reading the story, ask the children to imagine that they were able to speak to the fishes. What would they say to persuade them to leave the lake? They could discuss this in pairs. Following this, they could individually (with the teacher in role as one of the fishes) try as hard as they can to explain why it is important to leave.

Follow-up Activities
◆ Discuss the fact that frogs are amphibious, and live in the water and on land. What other facts can the children find out about frogs?

◆ With the children, come up with a list of things that can be classed as dangerous. Children could then create a poster which warns others about something dangerous.

Moral
Take notice when something seems dangerous.

The Tale of Two Fishes and a Frog

Reading Task A Write the words in the correct order.

1. frog upset. was The

   _____

2. The care. fishes did not

   _____

3. frog left The lake. the

   _____

4. men The fishes. caught the

   _____

Reading Task B Draw the two fishes and the frog in the lake.

The Tale of Two Fishes and a Frog

Circle True or False.

1. In the story there were three fishes.   True/False

2. The frog was worried when he saw the two men.
   True/False

3. The fishes were worried about the men coming back.   True/False

4. It took the men a long time to catch the two fish.
   True/False

Write what you think.

1. Do you think the frog gave the two fish good advice? Explain.

_____

_____

2. Did you like the way the story ended? Explain.

_____

_____

The Flying Turtle

Long ago there lived a turtle who wished that he could fly. One day, the turtle told an eagle about his wish. The eagle came up with a plan to help the turtle.

"I will hold you while I fly, so that you can see what it feels like," said the eagle.

The eagle grasped the turtle with his large claws, and soared up into the sky. The turtle felt happy up in the air. He began to feel like he could fly on his own.

"Let go – I can fly by myself!" shouted the turtle.

"Are you sure?" asked the eagle.

The turtle said yes, so the eagle let go. The turtle flapped his flippers – but this did not work. Poor turtle fell from the sky and landed on the ground with a smash. His shell cracked. From that day on, turtle never again tried to fly. He used his flippers to swim. At last, he had learned to be happy with who he was.

Teacher's Notes: The Flying Turtle

Background Information
A tale from India.

Words to Discuss Before Reading

turtle   Ask the children if they know what a turtle looks like. Can they explain the difference between a turtle and a tortoise? Show pictures of turtles and discuss features such as the shell and flippers.

eagle   Ask the children if they know what eagles are. Explain they are very large powerful birds which can be up to a metre in length, and have a wingspan of over two metres. Use a metre ruler to show size. Show pictures. Discuss features such as claws.

Speaking and Listening Activities
After reading the story, look at the first line. Ask the children if they can think of what they could say to turtle to convince him he does not need to fly. The teacher could then be in role as turtle and ask the children to convince turtle that it is fine not to be able to fly. Also the children could think of what they might say to turtle later on in the story when he says to eagle 'Let go – I can fly by myself!'

Follow-up Activities

◆   The children could draw and label pictures of turtles or/and eagles.

◆   Show children pictures of different turtle shells and ask them to design and then colour their own.

Moral
Learn to be content with what you have.

The Flying Turtle

Complete the answer to the question.

1. Who wanted to fly?
    T _ _ _ _ _ wanted to fly.

2. Who helped turtle?
    E _ _ _ _ helped turtle.

3. How did Turtle feel when he was in the air?
    Turtle felt h _ _ _ _ .

4. Where did turtle land when he fell?
    Turtle landed on the g _ _ _ _ _ .

Draw eagle trying to help turtle to fly.

Understanding Traditional Stories

The Flying Turtle

Reading Task **C** Draw lines to match the characters with what they did in the story The first one has been done for you.

The eagle	wished he could fly.
	had large claws.
	knew how to fly.
The tortoise	fell from the sky.
	had flippers.

Reading Task **D** Write what you think.

1. Explain how eagle tried to help turtle.

   _____

   _____

2. Why did eagle let go of turtle?

   _____

   _____

3. Why do you think turtle never again tried to fly?

   _____

   _____

The Singing Donkey

Once there lived a donkey and a fox who were friends. Both of them were quite naughty, and every night they would sneak into the fields of the local farmers and steal crops.

One night, they went to a cucumber field, and the donkey began to munch on the cucumbers. It was a lovely night: the moon was bright, the stars were sparkling and the cucumbers were tasty.

"I'm so happy right now that I'm going to sing!" said the donkey.

"Please don't... you will wake up the farmers!" begged the fox.

"You are just jealous because I have a great voice!" replied the donkey.

The donkey began to bray loudly. The fox did not want to get caught, so he ran off quickly. On hearing the noise, the farmers woke up and dashed down to the field. When they found the donkey, and saw that he had been eating the cucumbers, they beat him hard with big sticks. After his beating, the donkey limped home aching all over. He wished that he had listened to his friend.

Understanding Traditional Stories

Teacher's Notes: The Singing Donkey

Background Information

A fable from the Panchatantra: India.

Words to Discuss Before Reading

naughty to behave badly.

bray the loud harsh sound made by a donkey.

crops plants grown by farmers, for example, vegetables and fruits. It may be useful to specifically discuss cucumbers as these are the crops referred to in the story.

aching suffering from a dull pain.

Speaking and Listening Activities

After reading, discuss the beginning of the story, and the fact that the fox and the donkey were both quite naughty. Identify what they were doing that was wrong. Ask the children to discuss in pairs what they could say to the fox and the donkey to explain that their behaviour is wrong. Why shouldn't they steal? The children should then share their ideas individually.

Follow-up Activities

◆ Discuss the sounds made by different animals. The children could then create a list of animals with the sound each makes, for example cows moo, lions roar.

◆ The children could discuss, then sketch and label some of the different crops which can be grown on farms.

Moral

Think about what you say or do before doing it.

The Singing Donkey

Reading Task **A** Choose the correct words from the box to complete the sentences.

sticks	ran	sing	friends	farmers

1.   The donkey and the fox were f __ __ __ __ __ __.

2.   The donkey wanted to s __ __ __ .

3.   The fox r __ __ off.

4.   The donkey's singing woke up the f __ __ __ __ __ __ .

5.   The farmers beat the donkey with big s __ __ __ __ __ .

Reading Task **B** Draw the donkey and the fox in the cucumber field.

The Singing Donkey

Reading Task C Tick two boxes for each question.

1. Who was described as "quite naughty"?

   ☐ The donkey   ☐ The farmers   ☐ The fox

2. What would the donkey and the fox do each night?

   ☐ steal sweets   ☐ sneak into fields   ☐ steal crops

3) What did the donkey say to the fox?

   ☐ "You are jealous."   ☐ "I feel hungry."

   ☐ "I have a great voice."

Reading Task D Write what you think.

1. Why did the donkey want to sing? Explain.

   _____

   _____

2. Do you think the fox gave the donkey good advice? Explain.

   _____

   _____

3. Why did the farmers beat the donkey? Explain.

   _____

   _____

Abu Ali Counts his Donkeys

Abu Ali went to the fair and bought nine donkeys. He decided to ride one of the donkeys home while the other donkeys followed behind.

Off he went, down the dusty road and through the hills. When he was about halfway home, he thought it would be a good idea to check that all of the donkeys were still there. He turned around to count them.

"One, two, three, four, five, six, seven, eight ... oh no!" he said.

Just then his friend Musa came strolling by.

"Musa help me!" Abu Ali called. "I had nine donkeys. Now I only have eight. Help me find the missing donkey!"

His friend counted the donkeys and then laughed.

"Abu Ali," said Musa. "If you get off the donkey and count again I think you will find the answer!"

Do you know where the missing donkey is?

Teacher's Notes: Abu Ali Counts his Donkeys

Background Information
A story from the Middle East.

Words to Discuss Before Reading

fair   a place where people meet to buy and sell things. The children will be familiar with fairs linked to fairgrounds or rides or school summer or Christmas fairs.

strolling   walking in a relaxed manner, not hurrying.

Speaking and Listening Activities
After reading the story, discuss the question at the end. Can the children figure out where the missing donkey is? (Abu Ali was sitting on it while he counted, so forgot to include it.) Provide hints to encourage the children to work out the answer for themselves if needed. With teacher in role, as Abu Ali, ask the children to pretend they are his friend Musa and ask them what they would say to Abu Ali to explain his mistake.

Follow-up Activities

◆   This story could be used to help children practise counting, writing and spelling numbers one to ten.

◆   Explore counting songs, or look at books to do with counting. (*Fun with Number Rhymes for the Early Years*, published by Brilliant Publications is a valuable resource that will enhance the children's mathematical skills.)

Abu Ali Counts his Donkeys

Reading Task A Complete the answer to the question.

1. How many donkeys did Abu Ali buy?
    Abu Ali bought n __ __ __ donkeys.

2. Where did he buy the donkeys?
    He bought the donkeys at the f __ __ __ .

3. How many donkeys did Abu Ali count?
    He counted e __ __ __ __ donkeys.

4. What was the name of Abu Ali's friend?
    His friend was called M __ __ __ .

Reading Task B Draw Abu Ali on his donkey.

Abu Ali Counts his Donkeys

Reading Task C Put a tick by the correct answer.

1. The road is described as
   ☐ fair   ☐ long   ☐ dirty   ☐ dusty

2. Abu Ali stopped when he was halfway home to
   ☐ rest   ☐ talk to Musa   ☐ check his donkeys

3) When Abu Ali counted eight donkeys he was
   ☐ angry   ☐ worried   ☐ happy

4) Musa counted
   ☐ nine donkeys   ☐ eight donkeys   ☐ six donkeys

Reading Task D Write what you think.

1. Why do you think Abu Ali decided to ride one of the donkeys home?

   _____

   _____

   _____

2. What mistake did Abu Ali make when he counted eight donkeys?

   _____

   _____

   _____

Rabbit Catches the Sun

Rabbit was very unhappy! He looked angrily at the big foot prints in the mud. Each morning Rabbit went hunting as soon as he woke up ... but he could never find much to eat. These same footprints were there every morning. Rabbit decided that the prints must belong to a large animal that woke up earlier than him, and took most of the food. Rabbit came up with a plan.

"I will use a net to make a trap to catch this greedy animal," he said.

The morning after he had set his trap, Rabbit got up very early to see what he had caught. From a distance, Rabbit could see something very big and bright shining from his net. As he got closer to the net, he felt hotter and hotter. Rabbit soon realised he had not caught an animal but he had caught the Sun!

Rabbit knew the world needed the Sun, so he ran to the net to set the Sun free. When he opened the net, the Sun zoomed back up into the sky. But as Rabbit quickly ran away, the Sun burnt off most of Rabbit's long tail.

And this is why today, rabbits have very short tails!

Teacher's Notes: Rabbit Catches the Sun

Background Information
A Native American story.

Words to Discuss Before Reading

angrily   showing extreme displeasure or dislike about something. Ask the children to discuss whether they have ever felt angry. How might they look if they looked at someone or something angrily?

early   before the usual time of something.

earlier   before the expected time.

from a distance   from far away.

Speaking and Listening Activity
After reading the story, remind the children of the part where it states "Rabbit knew the world needed the sun." Do they agree that the world needs sun? Ask them to discuss this in pairs and then explain their thoughts.

Follow-up Activities

◆   Ask the children if they know what the sky looks like when the sun rises. Find pictures to show them this. The children could paint or use pastels to create their own picture of sunrise.

◆   What do the footprints of different animals look like? Use an image search on the Internet to show children pictures of different footprints. They could then try to guess what the animal in the story with the large prints might have been.

Rabbit Catches the Sun

Choose a word to finish the sentence.

trap	footprints	Sun	hunting	tail

1. Rabbit went h __ __ __ __ __ __ each morning.

2. Rabbit saw some f __ __ __ __ __ __ __ __ __ in the mud.

3. Rabbit set a t __ __ __ .

4. Rabbit caught the S __ __ .

5. The Sun burnt Rabbit's t __ __ __ .

Draw Rabbit before he lost his tail.

Understanding Traditional Stories

Rabbit catches the Sun

Reading Task C Write these events in the correct order.

Rabbit caught the Sun.
Rabbit set a trap.
Rabbit saw footprints.

_____

_____

_____

_____

_____

_____

Reading Task D Write what you think.

1. Rabbit describes the creature that made the footprints as greedy. Why does he use the word "greedy"? Explain.

_____

_____

_____

2. In the story it says "Rabbit knew the world needed the Sun". Do you agree? Explain.

_____

_____

_____

The Giant Turnip

Long ago, a grandfather planted a turnip. When it was time for the turnip to be pulled up, the grandfather grasped the turnip stalk and tugged hard. To his surprise, the turnip would not shift.

"Come and help me," he called to his wife.

She held onto her husband and pulled, but nothing happened.

"Come and help us!" she called to their granddaughter.

So the granddaughter pulled her grandmother, who pulled the grandfather who pulled the turnip ... but nothing happened.

The granddaughter called the dog. The dog pulled at the granddaughter, who pulled the grandmother, who pulled the grandfather, who pulled at the turnip – but still nothing! They even called the cat to help. The cat joined the chain. They all pulled – but still nothing happened. Finally, they saw a little mouse run by. Could a little mouse help?

They called the mouse. It pulled the cat, which pulled the dog which pulled the granddaughter, who pulled the grandmother, who pulled the grandfather, who pulled the turnip ...

It worked! At last the turnip came flying out. The animals and people in the chain fell backwards and landed in a heap. The turnip was gigantic. That night everyone enjoyed turnip soup. In fact, they enjoyed turnip soup every night for two whole weeks!

Teacher's Notes: The Giant Turnip

Background Information
A folk story from Russia.

Words to Discuss Before Reading
stalk main stem of a plant or attachment for a leaf. Show children a picture of a plant (you could show them a turnip plant) and identify the stalk.

grasped to hold onto something firmly.

gigantic something that is absolutely enormous.

Speaking and Listening Activity
After reading, ask the children if they can name the different characters in the story. In a group of six, assign each child a different character's role. Ask each of them to explain which part they did in the story.

Follow-up Activities

◆ What is a root vegetable? Create a list and draw and label some root vegetables.

◆ Discuss how to grow turnips, and other vegetables. If suitable, extend the work into actually planting and growing vegetables.

◆ Link to health. Discuss the importance of eating five fruit and vegetable each day. The children could make healthy eating posters promoting the benefits of eating vegetables.

The Giant Turnip

Reading Task A Choose the correct word from the box to complete the sentences.

grandmother		turnip	grandfather
mouse		dog	cat

1.   The grandfather planted a t _ _ _ _ _ .

2.   The grandmother pulled the g _ _ _ _ _ _ _ _ _ _ _ _ _ .

3.   The granddaughter pulled her g _ _ _ _ _ _ _ _ _ _ _ _ .

4.   The c _ _ pulled the d _ _ .

5.   The m _ _ _ _ pulled the c _ _ .

Reading Task B Draw a picture to show what happened at the end of the story.

Understanding Traditional Stories

The Giant Turnip

Reading Task **C** Circle True or False.

1. The turnip was easy to pull up. True/False

2. The grandfather called his wife to help him.
True/False

3. The mouse pulled the dog. True/False

4. The turnip was tiny. True/False

5. Nobody liked turnip soup. True/False

Reading Task **D** Write what you think.

1. Do you think the mouse could have pulled up the turnip on his own? Explain.

_____

_____

_____

2. Would you like to eat turnip soup for two weeks? Explain.

_____

_____

_____

The Greedy Lion

Lion was the king of the jungle. He ate lots of animals every day. The other animals begged him:

"Please – just eat one of us each day."

Lion agreed, but said that the animal to be eaten should come to find him. Each day an animal went to Lion to be eaten. Soon it was the turn of Hare - but Hare did not turn up. Lion went to look for him. He found him sitting by a well.

"Why did you not come to be eaten?" roared Lion.

"Because there is another lion down here who wants to eat me," said Hare looking into the well.

"No one takes my food!" yelled Lion.

Lion rushed to the well. Looking down into the water, he saw the lion. Angrily, Lion jumped into the well to fight him. Poor Lion drowned! He did not realise that the lion which he could see was his own reflection.

Understanding Traditional Stories

Teacher's Notes: The Greedy Lion

Background Information
A tale from Africa.

Words to Discuss Before Reading

hare   a creature that is very much like a rabbit, has longer limbs and ears and moves more quickly. If possible show the children pictures of hares.

well   a deep hole that is sunk in the ground which contains water. If needed show the children pictures of wells.

reflection   an image you get from looking in a mirror. Ask the children to look into mirrors and see their reflection. Explain that reflections can also be seen in water, shiny and glass surfaces etc.

Speaking and Listening Activity
The other creatures would have been very surprised to see Hare returning. What might Hare have said to them? In small groups the children could role-play the scene where Hare returns.

Follow-up Activities

◆   Discuss reflection and ask the children to work in pairs with one person mirroring the actions of the other. This could be done with reference to the last part of the story. For example, with one child acting as a lion (roaring or making a scary face) and the other mirroring their actions.

◆   Using a mirror to help them the children could draw their own reflections.

The Greedy Lion

Choose the correct words for the sentences

animals	eaten	king	jumped	well

1. Lion was k _ _ _ of the jungle.

2. Lion ate other a _ _ _ _ _ _ .

3. Each day an animal went to lion to be e _ _ _ _ .

4. Lion found Hare sitting by a w _ _ _ .

5. Lion j _ _ _ _ _ into the well.

Reading Task **B** Sketch and label some jungle animals.

Understanding Traditional Stories

The Greedy Lion

Circle True or False.

1.   Hare was king of the jungle.   True/False

2.   Each week an animal went to Lion to be eaten.
                                           True/False

3.   Hare went to find Lion.   True/False

4.   Hare wanted to fight Lion.   True/False

5.   Lion thought he saw another lion in the well.
                                           True/False

Write what you think.

1. Do you think the other animals liked Lion? Explain.

_____

_____

2. Why did Hare not go to find Lion?

_____

_____

3. Why did Lion jump into the water?

_____

_____

Tortoise and Baboon

Baboon invited Tortoise to lunch. It took Tortoise a long time to walk to where Baboon lived. When Tortoise arrived, he found Baboon sitting high up in a tree.

"The food is up here. Come and get it!" Baboon said.

As Tortoise could not climb a tree, he was not able to get any food. Baboon had tricked Tortoise. Tortoise was very upset. He decided to teach Baboon a lesson. He asked Baboon to come to lunch the next day.

When Baboon arrived, Tortoise told him to go to the river to wash his hands before eating. Baboon did as Tortoise asked. On his way back from the river his hands got dirty because the ground was so muddy.

"Go and wash your hands again," said Tortoise.

Baboon went back to the river to wash his hands – but the same thing happened. Baboon tried again and again. Each time, on his way back, the muddy ground made his hands dirty. In the end Baboon gave up and went home hungry. Tortoise had tricked Baboon.

Teacher's Notes: Tortoise and Baboon

Background Information
A tale from Africa.

Words to Discuss Before Reading

baboon   Check that the children know that a baboon is a type of monkey. Ask if they have ever seen one and show them pictures if needed.

invited   to be asked by someone to come somewhere. Ask the children if they have ever been invited for lunch, dinner or to a party. Have they ever invited anyone somewhere?

Speaking and Listening Activities
After reading the story, refer to the part of the story where Tortoise arrived for lunch and Baboon was up a tree. Ask the children to try to imagine what each character was thinking at this point. Arrange the children into pairs. Ask one child to be in role as Baboon and the other as Tortoise. The children should then take it in turns to speak their thoughts aloud.

Follow-up Activities

◆   Ask the children – why is it important to wash your hands before eating? The children could make a poster to remind people why it is important to wash their hands.

◆   What different types of monkeys have the children heard of? Find a picture of a baboon and another type of monkey (for example an orang-utan or a squirrel monkey). Ask the children to write sentences comparing similarities and differences between the monkeys.

Tortoise and Baboon

A Choose a word to finish the sentence.

lesson	wash	Tortoise	hungry	Baboon

1. B _ _ _ _ _ was sitting in a tree.

2. T _ _ _ _ _ _ _ could not climb a tree.

3. Tortoise wanted to teach Baboon a l _ _ _ _ _ .

4. Tortoise told Baboon to w _ _ _ his hands.

5. Baboon went home h _ _ _ _ _ .

Reading Task **B** Draw Baboon sitting high up in a tree and Tortoise down below on the ground.

Understanding Traditional Stories

Tortoise and Baboon

Reading Task C Draw lines to match the characters to what they did in the story

Tortoise	tricked Tortoise.
	walked to where Baboon lived.
	sat up in a tree.
Baboon	washed his hands in the river.
	tricked Baboon.

Reading Task D Write what you think.

1. Do you think Baboon behaved badly towards Tortoise? Explain.

_____

_____

2. Do you think Tortoise behaved badly towards Baboon? Explain.

_____

_____

3. What lesson do you think Baboon learned?

_____

_____

The Fox and the Tiger

A hungry tiger was walking in the forest when he saw a fox.

"I'm going to eat you up!" said the tiger licking his lips.

"You think that you are the king of the beasts – but you are not as scary as me!" said the fox.

The tiger was surprised, but the fox told him that he could prove that what he had said is true.

"Walk behind me," said the fox.

As the tiger walked, he noticed that all of the other animals looked terrified and ran off as soon as they saw the fox.

"It is true – you are scarier than me!" agreed the tiger.

The tiger began to feel quite nervous …
so he ran away too! The tiger did not
realise that the real reason the
other animals had run away was
because they could see that
he was behind the fox.

Teacher's Notes: The Fox and the Tiger

Background Information
A tale from China.

Words to Discuss Before Reading
prove to show something is true.

terrified very scared. Discuss the difference between scared and terrified.

nervous feeling uneasy and not relaxed. Ask the children if they have ever felt nervous or worried about something happening.

Speaking and Listening Activity
After reading the story, ask the children to imagine they are the fox. In role as the fox, they should explain what happened when they met tiger and how they tricked him.

Follow-up Activities
◆ Compare this Chinese folk story to *The Gruffalo* by Julia Donaldson. What similarities and differences are there?

◆ Make a list of the other animals that might have been in the forest.

The Fox and the Tiger

Reading Task **A** Complete the answer to the question.

1. Where was the tiger when he saw the fox?
The tiger was walking in the f __ __ __ __ __ .

2. Who felt hungry?
The t __ __ __ __ felt hungry.

3. Where did the fox tell the tiger to walk?
The fox told the tiger to walk b __ __ __ __ __ him.

4. Why did the tiger run away?
The tiger ran away because he felt n __ __ __ __ __ __ .

Reading Task **B** Draw a scene from the story.

Understanding Traditional Stories

The Fox and the Tiger

Reading Task C

Draw lines to match the characters with their actions. The first one has already been done.

The tiger	tricked the tiger.
The fox	that the fox was scarier.
The other animals	licked his lips.
The tiger agreed	because they saw the tiger.
The animals ran	looked terrified.

Reading Task D

Write what you think.

1. Do you think the other animals were really afraid of the fox?

   _____

   _____

2. Which animal do you think is more scary – a tiger or a fox? Explain.

   _____

   _____

3. Do you think it was mean of the fox to trick the tiger? Explain.

   _____

   _____

The Lion and the Jackal

Once long ago, a lion was walking in the mountains when he spotted a jackal. He decided to try to catch the jackal and eat him for his dinner!

The lion crept up to the jackal and went to pounce. He was very surprised to see that the jackal looked pleased to see him.

"I'm so glad you are here," said the jackal. "These rocks above our heads are about to fall. Please help to hold them up."

The lion followed the jackal's instructions. He stretched up and placed his paws onto the rocks.

"Great!" said the jackal. "Wait there – I will go and get a log to lean against the rocks to keep them in place."

The jackal ran off – but he did not come back. The lion waited for a long time. Eventually, he moved his paws and the rocks stayed in place and he realised the jackal had tricked him!

Understanding Traditional Stories

Teacher's Notes: The Lion and the Jackal

Background Information
A tale from Africa.

Words to Discuss Before Reading

jackal   a wild animal related to the dog family. Show the children a picture of a jackal and discuss differences between a lion and a jackal.

pounce   to jump quickly towards something in order to grab it. Often used to describe an animal catching its prey.

realise   develop understanding.

instructions   to follow orders on how to do something.

Speaking and Listening Activity
Imagine you are the jackal. Explain to a friend (this could be the teacher in role) how you stopped the lion from eating you.

Follow-up Activities

◆   Ask the children why they think the lion tried to eat the jackal. Discuss why the lion is known as the king of the jungle. Explain that in the wild many animals eat other animals to survive. Help the children to find out what lions eat and what jackals eat. Draw pictures which show the different diets of a lion and a jackal.

◆   Link to the Speaking and Listening Activity. The children could rewrite the story in role, as first person; either the lion or the jackal. Some modelling by the teacher may be needed for this.

The Lion and the Jackal

Reading Task A Choose the correct words to complete the sentences.

paws	rocks	ran	eat	tricked

1.   The lion wanted to e __ __ the jackal.

2.   The jackal told the lion the r __ __ __ __ were about to fall.

3.   The lion put his p __ __ __ on the rocks.

4.   The jackal r __ __ off.

5.   The jackal t __ __ __ __ __ __ the lion.

Reading Task B Draw the lion trying to hold up the rocks.

Understanding Traditional Stories

The Lion and the Jackal

Circle the correct answer.

1. The lion was walking in the …
   a) forest.   b) jungle.   c) mountains.   d) zoo.

2. The jackal asked the lion to hold up some …
   a) dinner.   b) rocks.   c) paws.   d) a log.

3) The jackal pretended to go and get …
   a) a log.   b) a rock.   c) a mountain.

4) The jackal …
   a) helped the lion.   b) fooled the lion.

Write what you think.

1. Would you describe the jackal as clever? Explain.

_____

_____

2. Would you describe the lion as clever? Explain.

_____

_____

3. Do you think it was wrong of the jackal to trick the lion? Explain.

_____

_____

The Fox and the Bagpipes

A fox was feeling hungry. He searched all over, but could find nothing to eat. Then he came across some bagpipes. The fox stared at the bagpipes and licked his lips.

Now you might think bagpipes are not food. And of course the pipes would be far too hard and crunchy to eat. But to the fox, the bag looked tempting because it was made from animal skin. The starving fox decided to eat the bag.

As the fox bit down on the bag, the movement of the air in the bag made the pipe give a long deep groan. Surprised by this, the fox stopped for a moment:

"Here is meat and music!" he said.

Then he munched on the bag, and enjoyed his meal which was very tasty indeed.

Teacher's Notes: The Fox and the Bagpipes

Background Information
A Scottish folk story.

Words to Discuss Before Reading

bagpipes   a musical instrument made with pipes and a bag. Show the children pictures of bagpipes, and if possible use the Internet to find video footage of them being played. Explain that they are often associated with Scotland.

tempting   attractive or appealing; when linked with food this word means you really like the look (or smell) of it and want to taste it.

Speaking and Listening Activity
After the story discuss the fact that the fox enjoyed his meal, and ask the children if they think the meal would be 'tempting' to them. Lead into a discussion on favourite meals. The children could discuss favourite meals in pairs and then feedback to the rest of the class/group.

Follow-up Activities

◆   Discuss the fact that this folk story is from Scotland. Show the children a map of the United Kingdom, and help them to identify Scotland, England and Wales. The children could be given their own copy of a the map and they could label appropriately. Extend with other map based activities, eg identifying where they live on a map.

◆   Use the story, to discuss how the bagpipe makes sounds, and then look at a selection of other musical instruments and discuss how they are used to create sounds.

The Fox and the Bagpipes

Reading Task **A** Write the words in the correct order.

1. hungry. was The fox

   _____

2. The licked his fox lips.

   _____

3. Bagpipes food. are not

   _____

4. fox bag. The ate the

   _____

Reading Task **B** Draw a picture of some bagpipes.
Label the bag and the pipes.

Understanding Traditional Stories

The Fox and the Bagpipes

Reading Task C Tick two boxes for each question.

1. Which words tell you the fox was hungry?

☐ licked his lips   ☐ surprised by this   ☐ The starving fox

2. Which words tell you the fox liked the taste of the bag?

☐ enjoyed his meal

☐ very tasty indeed

☐ the pipe made a long deep groan

Reading Task D Write what you think.

1. Why did the fox not want to eat the pipes?

_____

_____

_____

2. How do you think the owner of the bagpipes might feel
   when they find the pipes with no bag?

_____

_____

_____

Why the Emu has Short Wings

Long ago an emu was flying up high in the sky. He looked down and saw lots of birds gathered by a lagoon. He flew down to see what was going on.

The emu saw that the birds were all gathered around the brolga bird watching him dance. The brolga bird was a wonderful dancer. The emu wished that he could dance like the brolga bird.

"How could I learn to dance like you?" he asked the brolga bird.

The brolga bird did not want to teach any of the other birds to dance like him. He enjoyed being the centre of attention. He decided to trick the emu. The brolga bird made sure his wings were tucked in so it was hard to see them.

"You need short wings like me to be a good dancer," he told the emu. "Stand still and I will clip your wings for you."

How helpful the brolga bird is thought the emu. But after the emu wings were cut short – he found he still could not dance. Even worse, the emu found he could no longer fly! The brolga bird laughed at the emu, and then spread his wings and flew away. Poor emu, his wings never grew back. So now, emus cannot fly – but they are really fast runners!

Teacher's Notes:
Why the Emu has Short Wings

Background Information
A folk story from Australia.

Words to Discuss Before Reading

emu/brolga bird	Use the Internet to show the children pictures of the emu and the brolga bird which are native to Australia. Discuss their appearance.
gathered	brought together, assemble in a group.
lagoon	a small lake found near to a larger lake or a river.
centre of attention	the thing or person everyone is looking at or interested in.

Speaking and Listening Activities
After reading the story, refer back to the last paragraph. Ask the children how the emu might have felt when he discovered he still could not dance, and could no longer fly. What might the emu have said to the brolga bird? How might the brolga bird have answered? The children could imagine that the brolga bird and the emu have an argument about what has happened, and role-play this in pairs.

Follow-up Activities

◆ The children could research: birds, animals native to Australia or find out facts about the emu and the brolga bird.

◆ Using the Speaking and Listening Activity as a stimulus, the children could draw pictures with speech bubbles or write dialogue to show the argument.

Why the Emu has Short Wings

Reading Task A Fill in the blanks to complete the sentences.

| wonderful | runner | tricked |
| short | lagoon | |

1. There were lots of birds by the l _ _ _ _ _ .

2. The brolga bird was a w _ _ _ _ _ _ _ _ dancer.

3. The brolga bird t _ _ _ _ _ _ the emu.

4. The emu had his wings cut s _ _ _ _ .

5. The emu is a very fast r _ _ _ _ _ .

Reading Task Draw the emu before and after.

Why the Emu has Short Wings

Reading Task C Draw lines to match the characters with their descriptions.

The emu

The brolga bird

had his wings cut short

wished he could dance

was a wonderful dancer.

tricked the emu.

is a really fast runner.

Reading Task D Write what you think.

1. The brolga bird "enjoyed being the centre of attention". What does this mean? Explain.

_____

_____

2. Do you think the brolga bird behaved badly towards the emu? Explain.

_____

_____

3. How do you think the emu felt at the end of the story? Explain.

_____

_____

The Lizard and the Sun

Long, long ago, with no warning, the sun suddenly disappeared. The world was dark. The plants would not grow and it was cold. The people and the animals were unhappy. Where was the sun?

After searching for many days, the people and animals lost hope. They thought they would never find the sun. But the lizard would not give up. He searched high and low, until finally, he saw something bright and glowing in the sand. It was the sun – lying in the sand fast asleep!

Lizard ran to the king and told him what he had found. The king knew he had to wake up the sun quickly.

"I need music, dancers, and lots of food NOW!" he said.

The king told everyone there would be a festival in honour of the sun. The festival began. It was lively and loud. All the people and the animals in the land joined in. There was music, dancing and wonderful food. The sun woke up and zoomed up high into the sky. Once again, the world was warm and bright. And it was all thanks to the lizard who would not give up.

Teacher's Notes: The Lizard and the Sun

Background Information
A folk story from Mexico.

Words to Discuss Before Reading

disappeared something that was there has now gone.

search look for something/someone.

festival a celebration which often involves lots of people, music, food, dance. Festivals are often linked to religion. Ask the children if they know of any festivals eg, Divali.

honour to show someone/something great respect.

Speaking and Listening Activity
After reading the story, ask the children to think about how their life would be different if the sun disappeared. In pairs they should share their thoughts and then share ideas with the group/class.

Follow-up Activities

◆ There are many traditional folk stories linked to the sun. Compare this story with another folk story eg, Rabbit catches the Sun (pages 39–42). Compare similarities and differences.

◆ Use the Internet to find about facts about the sun.

The Lizard and the Sun

Reading Task A Choose the correct word from the box to complete the sentences.

give	cold	disappeared	asleep	sun

1. The sun d __ __ __ __ __ __ __ __ __ .

2. It was c __ __ __ .

3. Lizard would not g __ __ __ up.

4. Lizard found the s __ __ .

5. The sun was fast a __ __ __ __ __.

Reading Task B Draw the festival.

The Lizard and the Sun

Reading Task C   Tick two boxes for each question.

1. Which words describe the world when the sun disappeared?

   ☐ bright

   ☐ dark   ☐ cold

2. Which words describe the world after the sun was found?

   ☐ bright   ☐ lively

   ☐ warm

Reading Task D   Write what you think.

1. Why do you think the king wanted to wake up the sun quickly?

   _____

   _____

   _____

2. The lizard "would not give up". Explain what this means. Does this story has a happy ending?

   _____

   _____

   _____

The Elves and the Shoemaker

Long ago there lived a shoemaker and his wife. They were very poor. One day, the shoemaker found he only had enough leather left to make one pair of shoes. Before he went to bed, he cut the leather up, so that it would be ready to be sewn into shoes in the morning.

While the shoemaker and his wife slept, two little elves crept in. They sewed the leather up and made a beautiful pair of shoes. In the morning the shoemaker and his wife were amazed to see the shoes. They did not know who had made them.

A rich lady came into the shop.

"Wow!" she said. "I will pay you lots of money for these lovely shoes."

With the money from the rich lady, the shoemaker was able to buy lots more leather. Each night he cut out the leather, so that it was ready to be sewn. Each morning he woke to find wonderful shoes. Rich people came from far and wide to buy them. Soon the shoemaker and his wife became rich.

Teacher's Notes:
The Elves and the Shoemaker

Background Information
One of Grimm's fairy tales from Germany.

Words to discuss before reading

elves   often shown as small human like creatures with large pointed ears. In stories and tales they often try to help humans. Ask the children if they have heard of Santa's elves.

leather   a flexible hard wearing material (animal hide/skin) often used to make shoes.

Speaking and Listening Activities
After reading, ask the children what the shoemaker would have been thinking at the beginning of the story when he cut up his last piece of leather. The children should then speak his thoughts out loud in role. Next ask the children what the shoemaker would have been thinking when he came down the next morning and found the shoes made. They should again speak his thoughts out loud in role.

Follow-up Activities

◆   Ask the children what they think the cut out pieces of leather ready to be sewn into shoes looked like. They could draw the shape of the pieces they imagine onto paper.

◆   The shoes the elves make are described as beautiful, amazing and wonderful. Pupils could draw their own special shoes which they could colour, paint, add glitter to or even collage. Children could write written descriptions for their shoes.

◆   For a more extended project children could design and make their own shoes using materials.

The Elves and the Shoemaker

Reading Task A Write the words in the correct order.

1. elves Two in. crept

_____

2. elves made shoes. The

_____

3. beautiful. were The shoes

_____

4. A lady rich shoes. wanted the

_____

Reading Task B Draw pictures of the main characters.

Understanding Traditional Stories

The Elves and the Shoemaker

Reading Task C — Write the answer for each question.

1. Which words tell you that the shoemaker and his wife did not have a lot of money?

   _____

2. When did the shoemaker cut up the leather?

   _____

3. When did the elves come?

   _____

4. How did the shoemaker and his wife feel when they saw the shoes?

   _____

Reading Task D — Write what you think.

1. Explain how the elves helped the shoemaker and his wife become rich.

   _____

   _____

   _____

2. Why do you think lots of people came to buy the shoes?

   _____

   _____

   _____

The Elves and the Shoemaker (Rest of story)

One night, the shoemaker and his wife decided it was time to find out who was helping them. They stayed up and hid behind the curtains and waited. Soon, they saw the two little elves jump up onto the table and begin sewing. They worked hard all night, and then left as soon as the sun began to rise.

The shoemaker and his wife noticed the elves were dressed in rags. They wanted to reward the elves for their hard work so they made them some clothes.

The next night, when the elves arrived, they were very excited to find the outfits. They put on their new clothes and danced around happily. After that night, the elves were never seen again. The shoemaker and his wife lived happily ever after. They never forgot the kind elves who had helped them.

Understanding Traditional Stories

The Gingerbread Man

Once upon a time there lived a little old lady and a little old man. They were feeling hungry. The old lady decided she would make a gingerbread man.

First, she made the dough. Next she rolled it out flat. Carefully, she cut the dough into the shape of a gingerbread man. She gave him currants for eyes and chocolate chips for buttons. Finally, she popped the gingerbread man in the oven to bake.

When the gingerbread man was cooked, the old lady opened the oven. As she pulled out the tin, to her surprise, the gingerbread man jumped up.

"Don't eat me!" he shouted and ran out the door.

The old lady began to chase the gingerbread man.

"Run, run, as fast as you can! You can't catch me, I'm the gingerbread man!" he shouted.

Teachers' Notes: The Gingerbread Man

Background Information
A fairy tale from America.

Words to Discuss Before Reading

gingerbread man   ask children what a gingerbread man is and whether they have ever tasted one. The teacher could show pictures or bring one in.

dough   discuss whether the children have ever made biscuits. Explain that dough is the uncooked mixture of ingredients used to make biscuits, cake or bread.

Speaking and Listening Activity
After reading, ask the children what the old lady might have been thinking at different parts of the story. Choose specific parts and ask the children to speak their thoughts aloud in role as the old lady. For example, what is going through her mind while she is cooking or when the gingerbread man jumps up.

Follow-up Activities

◆ Find instructions for how to make a gingerbread man and explore how the recipe is set out. You could extend to looking at the features of other recipes.

◆ Make gingerbread men with the children.

The Gingerbread Man

Reading Task A Complete the answer to the question.

1. Who felt hungry?
The little old m __ __ and the little old l __ __ __ felt hungry.

2. Why did the old lady decide to make?
She decided to make a g __ __ __ __ __ __ __ __ __ __ __ __ / __ __ __ .

3. What did she use to make his eyes?
She used c __ __ __ __ __ __ __ to make his eyes.

4. What did she use to make buttons?
She used c __ __ __ __ __ __ __ __ / __ __ __ __ __ for buttons.

Reading Task B Draw the old lady chasing the gingerbread man.

The Gingerbread Man

Reading Task C Draw lines to match the characters with what they did in the story.

The old lady	shouted, "Don't eat me!"
	opened the oven.
	cut out the dough
The gingerbread man	chased the gingerbread man
	jumped up

Reading Task D Write what you think.

1. Do you think it would be surprising to see a gingerbread man running? Explain why.

   _____

   _____

   _____

2. Why did the old lady chase after the gingerbread man? Explain.

   _____

   _____

   _____

Understanding Traditional Stories

The Gingerbread Man (Rest of story)

The gingerbread man ran past a duck, a pig, a cow and a horse. They all gave chase.

"Run, run as fast as you can. You can't catch me, I'm the gingerbread man!" he shouted.

The animals and the little old lady chased him down to a river. On the river bank lay a fox.

"Do you want some help?" said the fox licking his lips.

The gingerbread man knew he could not swim across on his own. The animals and the little old lady were getting closer.

"Yes please!" said the gingerbread man.

He hopped onto the fox's back and the fox began to swim across.

"Hop onto my head little man – the water is getting deep!" said the fox.

The ginger bread man did not want to get wet so he hopped onto the fox's head. Quickly, the fox flipped his head upwards sending the gingerbread man flying up into the air. The gingerbread man fell down - right into the open mouth of the fox. Snap! That was the end of the gingerbread man!

The Magic Porridge Pot

A poor hungry girl went for a walk in the woods. There she met an old lady who gave her a magic pot. She told the girl that when she felt hungry she should just say "cook pot cook", and the pot would make porridge. To stop the porridge cooking she told the girl she would need to say "stop pot stop!"

The girl took the pot home. Her mother was delighted because the pot meant they would not have to worry about food again.

One day the girl went to visit her grandmother. While she was gone, the mother felt hungry so she said "cook pot cook". The pot made porridge, but the mother could not remember the words needed to make the pot stop cooking.

The porridge flowed out of the pot – onto the floor – out of the door – down the street – into houses - and all over the village. Everyone began to panic. The little girl walking home saw the porridge everywhere and guessed what had happened.

"Stop pot stop!" yelled the girl.

Immediately, the porridge stopped flowing. That day, anyone who wanted to get across town had to eat their way there!

Teacher's notes: The Magic Porridge Pot

Background Information
A fairy tale from Germany.

Words to Discuss Before Reading

porridge   rolled oatmeal or other cereal boiled with milk or water. Ask the children if they have ever tasted it.

panic   to quickly feel scared and or very nervous.

delighted   really happy.

immediately   straight away, at once.

Speaking and Listening Activities
After reading, discuss the part of the story where everyone began to panic. Why were they panicking? What might they have been thinking/worried about? Get the children to role-play this part of the story speaking their thoughts aloud.

Follow-up Activities
◆   Discuss porridge, what is it made of, how to cook it and when it is usually eaten. Consider whether porridge is viewed as a healthy food or unhealthy food. What other breakfasts and foods are viewed as healthy or unhealthy? Get the children to create a list.

◆   Make porridge with the children. Experiment with adding different toppings.

The Magic Porridge Pot

Reading Task A Write the words in the correct order.

1. girl The met old lady. an

_____

2. a pot. The old lady girl gave the

_____

3. pot The magic. was

_____

4. porridge. The made pot

_____

Reading Task B Draw the porridge all over the village.

Understanding Traditional Stories

The Magic Porridge Pot

Reading Task **C** Write the answer for each question.

1. Which words made the porridge cook?

   _____

2. Which words made the porridge stop cooking?

   _____

3. Who did the girl go to visit?

   _____

4. What did the girl see when she was walking home?

   _____

Reading Task **D** Write what you think.

1. Why did the villagers panic? Explain.

   _____

   _____

   _____

2. Would you have tried to eat your way across town or stayed at home? Explain why.

   _____

   _____

   _____

The Three Billy Goats Gruff

Long ago there lived three hungry billy goat brothers called Gruff. Near to where they lived was a hill full of lovely green grass. They all wanted to eat this grass, but to get to the hill they needed to cross a river. And under the bridge which crossed the river there lived a scary troll.

The three hungry billy goats decided to try to creep across the bridge one at a time. The smallest billy goat Gruff went first. Trip-trap went his noisy hooves as he crossed. The troll jumped out – ready to gobble him up.

"Wait! Another billy goat is coming soon and he is bigger than me. Eat him not me!" cried the smallest billy goat Gruff.

The troll agreed to wait. Soon it was time for the second billy goat. Trip-trap went his hooves loudly. The troll jumped out – ready to gobble him up.

"Wait for the last billy goat. He is even bigger still. Eat him not me!" cried the medium-sized billy goat Gruff.

The troll agreed to wait. Soon he heard the third billy goat try to cross. Trip-trap boomed his hooves across the bridge. The troll jumped out ready to gobble him up – but he got a shock. The third billy goat was huge! The biggest billy goat Gruff charged into the troll with his horns and sent him flying far away over the hill, and the troll was never seen again!

Teachers' Notes: The Three Billy Goats Gruff

Background Information
A Norwegian fairy story.

Words to Discuss Before Reading

billy goat   Show the children pictures of billy goats and discuss features including horns and hooves.

troll   In fairy tales trolls are often scary ugly creatures who are mean to others. If suitable, use the Internet to show the children pictures of trolls.

medium   discuss sizes. What is meant by medium?

Speaking and Listening Activity
After reading, discuss the behaviour of the troll. Ask the children what they might say to the troll to persuade him to change his behaviour and attitude to others. With teacher in role (as the troll) get the children to talk to the troll, trying to persuade him to be nicer to others.

Follow Up Activities

◆ Find out more about billy goats. The children could then draw and label pictures or write a report about them.

◆ Look at superlatives, eg big, bigger, biggest, small, smaller, smallest. Get the children to draw pictures of objects to match superlatives.

The Three Billy Goats Gruff

Reading Task A Choose the correct word from the box to complete the sentences.

hungry	troll	out	Gruff	grass

1.   The billy goats were called G _ _ _ _ .

2.   The billy goats felt h _ _ _ _ _ .

3.   The billy goats wanted to eat g _ _ _ _ .

4.   Under the bridge lived a t _ _ _ _ .

5.   The troll jumped o _ _ .

Reading Task B Draw the scary troll.

The Three Billy Goats Gruff

Reading Task **C** Circle the correct answer.

1. The troll lived …
    a) in the river.   b) on the hill.   c) under the bridge.

2. The medium sized billy goat crossed the bridge …
    a) first.   b) second.   c) last.

3) The last billy goat to cross was …
    a) small   b) medium sized   c) huge

4) The noise made by the billy goats' hooves went …
    a) trip-trop   b) trip-trap   c) trap-trip

Reading Task **D** Write what you think.

1. Explain why the troll did not eat the first billy goat.

    _____

    _____

    _____

2. Explain why the troll did not eat the third billy goat.

    _____

    _____

    _____

The Ugly Duckling

Long ago on a farm, a duck sat on her nest. She was waiting for her eggs to hatch. At last, the eggs began to crack and five pretty little ducklings popped out. That left just one egg to crack. This egg was bigger than the rest. Sadly, the mother duck sat back down on the egg. It would not hatch and she was fed up of waiting.

Finally, the egg cracked open … and out came a very strange duckling. It was not little and yellow. It was large and grey. The other ducklings stared at it. They began to laugh.

"How ugly he is," said one duckling.

"He is not like us – he is different," said another.

"Leave him alone," said the mother duck.

Her children took no notice. They teased the ugly duckling. To make matters worse, all of the other animals on the farm did the same. This teasing made the ugly duckling so sad that after a few months he decided to fly away.

Understanding Traditional Stories

Teacher's Notes: The Ugly Duckling

Background Information
A Danish fairy tale by Hans Christian Andersen.

Words to Discuss Before Reading

strange   something that is out of the ordinary, not what was expected.

different   not the same as others.

teasing   making fun of someone. Explain that teasing can mean to make fun of someone because they are different and that it can be hurtful. The children will probably be familiar with this word, allow them to discuss their interpretations.

Speaking and Listening Activity
After reading the story, ask the children to imagine they are able to speak to the other ducklings and the farm animals who teased the ugly duckling. What could they say to them to make them understand their behaviour is wrong?

Follow-up Activities

◆   Explain that some creatures look very different when they are first born, and then as they grow up (eg frogs, butterflies). Show pictures which show animals and their babies or life-cycles and compare and discuss.

◆   Ask the children to think of and discuss how different they were as a baby to how they are now.

The Ugly Duckling

Complete the answer to the question.

1. Who sat on her nest?
    A d _ _ _ sat on her nest.

2. Why did the mother duck sit on her nest?
    She was waiting for her e _ _ _ to hatch.

3. What colour was the ugly duckling?
    The ugly duckling was g _ _ _ .

4. How did the ugly duckling feel when he was teased?
    The ugly duckling felt s _ _ .

Draw pictures which show the ducklings.

The ugly duckling   All the other ducklings

The Ugly Duckling

Write these events in the correct order.

Five of the eggs hatched.
The biggest egg would not hatch.
The mother duck sat on her nest.

_____

_____

_____

_____

_____

_____

Write what you think.

1. Do you think the other ducklings and farm animals behaved badly towards the ugly duckling? Explain how.

_____

_____

_____

2. What do you think you should do if you are teased?

_____

_____

_____

The Ugly Duckling (Rest of story)

The ugly duckling flew over the wall of the farm. He soon found out life outside the farm was very scary. There were horrible men with guns who hunted birds. There were large dogs and cruel cats. The duckling found it hard to find a safe place to rest.

The poor duckling felt so unhappy. He was scared of being eaten or killed. He had no friends and felt lonely. And he found that even outside of the farm, other animals laughed at him and teased him still.

Autumn passed and winter came. It was so cold, snowy and icy that the poor duckling almost died. Spring came at last. The sun began to shine. The trees began to blossom. Life was easier.

The duckling felt stronger. He flew around looking for other birds – looking for friends. The duckling found a lake. On the lake he saw the most beautiful birds he had ever seen. They were swans. The duckling wished that he could be as beautiful as they were. He wondered if these swans would like to be his friends.

Slowly, the duckling approached the lake. When he reached the water, he looked down at his reflection. And guess what was there? The duckling had changed. He was ugly no more. The duckling saw looking back from the water - a swan! Entering the lake, he swam towards the other swans. They turned to look and their eyes seemed to say hello and welcome. The beautiful swan that had so often been told he was an ugly duckling had found happiness at last.

Cinderella

Once upon a time, there lived a beautiful girl called Cinderella. She lived with her horrible stepmother and her two ugly stepsisters. Her stepmother and stepsisters did not like Cinderella, and made her do all of the housework. Poor Cinderella!

One day an invitation arrived. It said that there was going to be a ball at the palace and everyone was invited.

"You cannot go," said the horrible stepmother to Cinderella.

"You have too much work to do!"

Cinderella was very upset. When her stepmother and stepsisters left to go to the ball, she began to cry. Suddenly, there was a flash of light and a kind looking lady appeared in front of her. It was her Fairy Godmother.

"I will help you to go to the ball!" she said.

Teacher's Notes: Cinderella

Background Information
The popular version of this fairy tale originates in France and was written by Charles Perrault

Words to Discuss Before Reading

invitation   Ask whether any of the children have ever received an invitation. What was it for? Who was it from? How did they feel when they received it?

suddenly   Explain that this word is often used in stories to show that something unexpected or surprising is about to happen.

appeared   something that was not there before that comes into sight. Challenge the children to explain the meaning of the opposite word – disappeared.

Speaking and Listening Activity
After reading, give the children the following instructions – pretend you are Cinderella. Your stepmother and stepsisters go off to the ball leaving you all alone. What are you thinking at this moment? State your thoughts aloud.

Follow-up Activities

◆   Write a list of all the things Cinderella might have had to do to help out around the house.

◆   How do you imagine the palace? Draw a picture of it.

Cinderella

Reading Task **A** Fill in the missing words to complete the sentences.

beautiful	palace	Godmother	ball	ugly	upset

1. Cinderella was b _ _ _ _ _ _ _ _ .

2. Cinderella had two u _ _ _ stepsisters.

3. There was going to be a ball at the p _ _ _ _ _ .

4. Cinderella was u _ _ _ _ because she wanted to go to the b _ _ _.

5. Cinderella's Fairy G _ _ _ _ _ _ _ _ came to help her.

Reading Task **B** Draw a picture of Cinderella and her two stepsisters.

Cinderella

Reading Task **C** Circle True or False.

1. Cinderella was ugly.   True/False

2. The stepsisters helped with the housework.   True/False

3. Everyone was invited to the ball.   True/False

4. The evil stepmother told Cinderella she
   could go to the ball.   True/False

5. The fairy Godmother told Cinderella that
   she would help her.   True/False

Reading Task **D** Write what you think.

1. Do you think it was wrong for the stepmother to say
   Cinderella could not go to the ball? Why?

   _____

   _____

   _____

2. Do you think it was right that Cinderella should have
   been made to do all the housework? Why?

   _____

   _____

   _____

Understanding Traditional Stories

Cinderella (Rest of story)

Cinderella's Fairy Godmother could do magic. She turned a pumpkin into a coach. After that, she turned some mice into horses and a rat into a coachman. Finally, she turned the rags Cinderella was wearing into a beautiful dress and made pretty glass slippers appear on her feet. Excitedly, Cinderella climbed into the coach.

"Be home before midnight!" her Fairy Godmother shouted after her as the coach drove off.

Cinderella had a wonderful time at the ball. She danced with the prince all night... until she heard the clock strike twelve. When Cinderella heard the chimes, she ran away. As she ran, one of her glass slippers fell off...

The prince was upset because he had fallen in love with Cinderella, and she had run off leaving only a glass slipper. Luckily he had an idea. He would search the kingdom to find the girl whose foot would fit the glass slipper.

The Prince looked all over until he found Cinderella. Of course, the glass slipper fitted her perfectly.

"Will you marry me?" he asked.

Cinderella said yes. She left her old life behind and she and the Prince married. They both lived happily ever after.

Goldilocks and the Three Bears

Once upon a time there lived three bears: a great big daddy bear, a medium sized mummy bear and a little baby bear. They lived in a pretty cottage in the woods. Each morning Mummy Bear would make porridge for breakfast. The porridge was always too hot to eat when it was first made. So the bears would go out for a walk while it cooled down.

One day, a little girl called Goldilocks was walking in the woods. She saw the bear's cottage. I wonder who lives there, she thought. She went to the door and pushed it open. There on the table were three bowls of porridge.

Yum! Goldilocks thought. Seeing noone, she went inside and ate a spoonful from the biggest bowl.

"Ouch!" she screamed. "This porridge it too hot!"

Next she went to the medium sized bowl and ate a spoonful.

"Yuck!" she screamed. "This porridge is too cold!"

Finally, she went to the smallest bowl and ate a spoonful.

"Yes!" she said happily. "This is just right!"

Goldilocks ate up all of the porridge in the small bowl.

Teachers' Notes:
Goldilocks and The Three Bears

Background Information
A fairy tale from England.

Words to discuss before reading

porridge   rolled oatmeal or other cereal boiled with milk or water. Ask the children if they have ever tasted it.

medium   discuss sizes. What is meant by medium?

cottage   a small old-fashioned cosy house usually found in a rural location. Ask the children if they think a house is different from a cottage.

Speaking and Listening Activity
After reading the story, develop a debate around the behaviour of the main character. Ask children to discuss in pairs 'Was Goldilocks naughty? Did she do anything wrong?' After discussion the children could share their ideas with the group/class.

Follow-on Activities

◆   Ask the children what routine the bears followed each morning. (The teacher may need to explain the word routine.) The children could discuss their own morning routines and make a list of the different things they do before they come to school.

◆   The children could draw and then paint/colour a picture of a pretty cottage in the woods.

◆   Discuss what Goldilocks did wrong. The children could then write a letter of apology to the bears from Goldilocks.

Goldilocks and The Three Bears

Complete the answer to the question.

1.   Where did the bears live?
The bears lived in a c __ __ __ __ __ __.

2.   What did the bears like to eat for breakfast?
The bears liked to eat p __ __ __ __ __ __ __.

3.   How many bowls of porridge were on the table?
There were t __ __ __ __ bowls of porridge on the table.

4.   Where were the bowls of porridge?
The bowls of porridge were on the t __ __ __ __.

Draw an illustration which shows an event from the story.

Understanding Traditional Stories

Goldilocks and The Three Bears

Reading Task C — Circle the correct answer.

1. The porridge was made by:
   a) Baby Bear   b) Daddy Bear   c) Mummy Bear

2. Goldilocks thought the big bowl of porridge was:
   a) too hot   b) too cold   c) just right

3) When Goldilocks tried the middle bowl she said ...
   a) "Yum!"   b) "Ouch!"   c) "Yuck!"

4) Goldilocks ate up all the porridge in the
   a) small bowl   b) big bowl   c) medium sized bowl

Reading Task D — Write what you think

1. Do you think it was wrong of Goldilocks to go into the cottage? Explain.

   _____

   _____

   _____

2. Do you think it was wrong for Goldilocks to eat all of the porridge?

   _____

   _____

After eating the porridge, Goldilocks felt tired. She wanted to sit down. She sat down on the biggest chair but did not like it.

"This chair is too hard!" she said.

She sat down on the medium sized chair but did not like it.

"This chair is too soft!" she said.

She sat down on the smallest chair but she was too big for it.

The chair broke and Goldilocks fell onto the floor.

"Bother!" she said.

Goldilocks was still tired, so she went upstairs to lie down. After trying all the beds, she decided the smallest bed was the most comfortable. She lay down and fell asleep.

While she was sleeping, the bears came back home. They saw that someone had eaten up all of Baby Bear's porridge. They saw that someone had sat on Baby Bear's chair – and broke it! Baby Bear cried. Mummy Bear was upset.

Daddy Bear roared, "Who has done this?"

He stomped upstairs and the other bears followed. When Daddy Bear saw Goldilocks sleeping on Baby Bear's bed, he roared loudly. Goldilocks woke up in a fright. When she saw the three bears, she jumped up and ran out of the cottage as fast as she could. The bears never saw Goldilocks again.

Understanding Traditional Stories

The Three Little Pigs

Once upon a time, there were three little pigs. The time came for them to leave home, so the pigs packed their bags and set out to seek their fortunes.

They came upon a pretty forest which was filled with flowers. The pigs thought it would be the perfect place to live. Each of them decided to build a house in the forest.

The first little pig did not like to work too hard. He decided to build his house quickly out of straw. It took him just one day to build it.

The second little pig was prepared to work a bit harder. He built his house carefully out of sticks. It took him two days.

The third pig wanted to build a house that would last. He was prepared to work very hard to make a strong house. He built a sturdy house out of bricks. It took him a whole week.

For a while, the pigs were happy in their houses. But one day a big, bad wolf came to the forest....

Teacher's Notes: The Three Little Pigs

Background Information
A fairy tale from England.

Words to Discuss Before Reading

seek their fortune The pigs in this story search for a future filled with happiness, comfort and success.

prepared ready for something.

sturdy very strong and firm.

Speaking and Listening Activity
After reading the story, ask the children to consider why it would not be a good idea to build a house quickly out of straw and sticks. They should then imagine they could speak to the first and second pig. What would they say if they could give them advice before they built their houses?

Follow-up Activities

◆ Link to science and the properties of materials. Discuss the materials used for the houses – which was best and why? Extend to discussion of other materials.

◆ The children could imagine they are going to build a house and create a design (outside only). After they have drawn the house ask the children to label the materials they would choose for the door, windows, walls and roof. They should then discuss the properties of the materials chosen eg, why use glass for windows?

The Three Little Pigs

Fill in the missing words.

1. Who built their house from straw?
   The f _ _ _ _ pig built their house from straw.

2. Who built their house from sticks?
   The s _ _ _ _ _ pig built their house from bricks.

3. Who built their house from bricks?
   The t _ _ _ _ pig built their house from bricks.

4. Who came to the forest?
   A big, bad w _ _ _ .

Draw one of the houses from the story.

Give your house a title. _____

The Three Little Pigs

Reading Task **C** Tick two boxes for each question.

1. The first pig built his house

☐ quickly   ☐ carefully   ☐ out of straw

2. The second pig built his house

☐ in a day   ☐ carefully   ☐ in two days

3) The third pig wanted to build a house that was

☐ big   ☐ strong   ☐ sturdy   ☐ old

4) The wolf is described in this part of the story as

☐ big   ☐ grey   ☐ bad   ☐ mad

Reading Task **D** Write what you think.

1. If you were building a house, would you rush or take your time? Explain why.

_____

_____

_____

2. Is straw a good material to build a house with? Explain why.

_____

_____

_____

The Three Little Pigs (Rest of the story)

The big bad wolf was hungry. He knocked at the door of the house made of straw.

"Little pig, little pig – let me in!" he growled.

"Not by the hair of my chinny, chin, chin!" replied the first pig.

"Then I'll huff and I'll puff and I'll blow your house down!" roared the wolf.

The wolf huffed and puffed and blew the house down.

The first little pig ran to his brother's house which was made out of sticks. But the wolf followed him. And he huffed and puffed and blew the stick house down as well!

The two pigs ran to their brother's house which was made out of bricks. The wolf chased after them. He huffed, and

The Three Little Pigs (Rest of the story)

he puffed, and he tried his very best to blow down the brick house. But the house was so strong the wolf could not blow it down.

The wolf thought of a new plan. He decided to creep down the chimney. However, the third pig was very clever. He guessed what the wolf was going to do, so he lit a fire. As the wolf crept down the chimney, his long tail dangled down into the flames below him.

"Ouch!" he screeched and scrambled back up the chimney with his tail on fire! The wolf jumped off the roof, and ran away from the brick house as fast as he could.

The little pigs never saw the big bad wolf again. From that day on, all three pigs lived together, safe and happy in the sturdy house made of bricks.

Lightning Source UK Ltd.
Milton Keynes UK
UKHW05f0430090418
320671UK00002B/24/P